The **Ways** of VALUABLE People

The **Ways** of Valuable People

UFOMADU
CONSULTING & PUBLISHING LLC

Dr. Udo F. Ufomadu

ISBN **978-0-9790022-4-3**

OTHER BOOKS WRITTEN BY UDO UFOMADU

5 Essential Habits

Anthology of Inspiration

Be Blessed

How to Become Extremely Successful in Business Management, Personal Management, and Family Budget Planning

Secrets of Elevation Hidden in Stirring Poems

Light

Quote the Best Out of You

TABLE OF CONTENTS

ACKNOWLEDGEMENT

-To God be all the glory for using me.

-To all biological and spiritual families; my pastor and mentors who teach, support, and pray for me.

- To past and present colleagues, past and present superintendents, and past /present employees of Selma City School who understand the importance overall learning.

- To some African, European, US, and Dallas county residents whom I have admired and learned from.

-To past and present employees of Department of Agriculture and Industries who are friends and supporters.

-To past and present employees at R. L. Ziegler Inc. who are friends and supporters.

-To all my friends who are always there for my family and I.

-To my parents for showing me the way to go when I was younger.

- To UC&P World Changing Books editors and officials.

INTRODUCTION

It is essential to realize that we are valuable indeed and constantly celebrate that fact regardless of what another opinion suggests. Most time, it is not that people doubt the fact that they are valuable or not; rather, it is wrong positioning that builds doubts, probably, through what is constantly read, watched, listened to and associated with.

Before positioning yourself to be constantly influenced through what I call external factors, it is imperative that you exhaust your internal factors which are centered on you as a person with capabilities, a soul, and a mind. How you feel; what you believe; and what you respect will go a long way to determine your exquisiteness, your valuableness, and your costliness.

Human beings tend to do things or have ways that agree with how they perceive themselves. If you perceive yourself to be valuable in every setting, there's no doubt that you will always carry yourself accordingly. In the process of trying to remain valuable, you could be misunderstood and consequently called derogatory names; but do not let that stop you from being the useful one because there is a reward for being valuable. Even if your action or your rationale for doing a certain thing is misunderstood, still that should never change the wise decision that you made to be helpful by activating your gifts and thereby remaining valuable.

When you are forced to keep your gift inside of you without bringing it out, everybody loses. Your gifts are not just for your personal admiration but for your community and beyond; more so, to people less fortunate than you. The kings, Queens, and king makers will never hear about your gift until you bring it out. Sometimes, fear of making mistakes or failing deter people from showing their gifts. Start helping with and sharing your gift with people that you are very comfortable with and I assure you that Kings and king makers who just need insight regardless of where it comes from will send for you regardless of what makes you different .In all, you do not have to set a time for the Kings to know about you and just remember that those that have mastered their patience to wait on God's time have perfected their success.

People usually do not wake up each morning and chase mistakes, still mistake occurs. Everything that we do or did may not have been how Almighty wants it but still we are precious. We should not have room or time to sit around and constantly feel bad about our past mistakes to the point that it does take away the energy needed for maximizing our potential as valuable people.

Do not let everything that you do be self-centered or based on what you can gain. If your ways or plans are saturated with only personal gains, it shows a deficient or skewed goal and plan. There may be good reason to do things that just help only others. Sometimes, our assignments from the Almighty look burdensome but it is only when the weight on you is not just from your personal load, but about fighting so that others will have what you already have, or not be denied like you were denied, that's when you maximize your valuableness. I wrote poems that are very much in harmony with this book.

VALUABLE INDEED

We will assuredly enjoy all

The days of our lives

Responding well to good deeds call

As relevance from many parts thrives

I am what Almighty and I said

Good dear precious and valuable

Esteemed is how we are made

Great cherished prized and reliable

We must eat the fruits of our labor

Harvesting from the seeds we did sow

Cups run over reapers gleam with vigor

Grateful songs will play river of joy will flow

GOD BLESS YOU

My family and I prayed

We asked God to help us

We asked God to help your family

And we believed in His Capability

We asked for His guidance

We prayed that He protect our homes

We prayed for our schools, leaders, and churches

And we believed in His ability.

We asked Almighty to bless all of us

Every day and surely in every way

We prayed that He forgive all of us

And we believed in His grace.

INSPIRATION

I hold fast the instruction of a heavenly father:

When the plan has not materialized

HOPE

When materialization takes longer

COPE

When the enemy whispers a lie

NOPE

Let's fetch from the prosperity stream that flows steadily:

When prophecy bell rings of your prosperity

BELIEVE

When the entire stream is ordered to overflow

RECEIVE

When heaven sends a perfect container

RELIEF

I found refuge in a supernatural that changes not:

When friends and mentors act like enemies

PRAY

When an innocent child surprises the devil

PRAISE

When all God's children have one enemy

"PRAYPRAISE"

Chapter 1

WHO ARE THE VALUABLE PEOPLE?

We are all valuable people. Because we are human beings, our conditions are not permanent. As a result, we strive to remain valuable individuals as our varied situations permit. What is more important is learning how to remain firm on positions that make you valuable or adjust appropriately in times of imperfection and challenges so as to still remain valuable. The following information may be helpful in our positioning.

_____Valuable people wear Peace like a badge. They wear it at home, at work, in school, in their communities, and outside of their communities.

_____You are valuable if you are missed each time that you are absent from your group. You are missed as a result of tangible and intangible assets that you bring to the table.

_____Valuable people build a community where hatred is sin; where weaknesses are not ridiculed but helped; where peace makers are crowned regularly.

_____You are valuable if you constantly work hard to expand your friendship network instead of expanding your enmity network because valuable people prefer to be your friend than to be your enemy.

_____You are valuable if you consider your group's success to be your success and your community's failure to be your failure.

_____The valuable voice says, if you take care of others, I will take care of you but the questionable voice tells you to take care of just yourself.

_____You are valuable if your humility is constant and not based on circumstances.

_____Valuable people realize that poverty of money or material possessions does not result from giving or sharing. You cannot be poor because you gave to those less privileged than you.

_____It is impossible to be of no value if go about solving other people's problem as much as you can.

_____You are valuable if you borrow and try to pay back.

_____Valuable people waste no time or energy in evil plotting or revenge but utilize the time in improving self and others; for that's where true gains abound.

____Regardless of position or title, you should never ignore a pressing issue that asks for your help simply because the chain of command was ignored or other. You are more valuable and honorable when you help outside of normal expectations.

____You are valuable if you are a grateful and a humble person who does not take credit for all the good things happening around you.

____Valuable people give more than they take.

____You are valuable if you also see the good done to you and not only the bad.

____You are valuable if you pray for your group even if you believe that a person in the group or the entire group did you wrong.

____When valuable people come around you, they show up with either one or all of these- hope, love, encouragement, peace, or joy.

____Check out this valuable piece, "I come that they may have life, and that they may have it more abundantly." --Jesus Christ

_____You are valuable if you always wait for God's appointed time for materialization to arrive, knowing fully well that your patience will be to everybody's benefit.

_____You are valuable if you believe in adjusting yourself if the problem that you are trying to solve refuses to adjust.

_____A valuable line postulates, "Ask not what your country can do for you, ask what you can do for your country" –JFK

_____A valuable quote confirms, "Intelligence plus character- that is the goal of true education." –MLK

_____"Focusing your life solely on making a buck shows a poverty of ambition. It asks too little of yourself" --B. Obama

_____You are valuable if you are just productive.

_____You are valuable if you are very convinced that there will always be a problem to solve in this world; for life is made to be challenging.

_____You are valuable in your group if you believe that the devil's obstructive machines will never deter a success of God's predestined.

____You are valuable if you believe that forgiveness will clean negative buildups, giving way for prosperity to abound.

____You are valuable if you fear God, not man.

____You are valuable if you certainly believe that success is not tied to luck.

____You are valuable if you know that the mastery of relationship with the owner of what you want should come first before the mastery of what he or she owns.

____You are valuable if you utilize your votes during elections or other opportunities to elect valuable and God fearing leaders.

____You are valuable if you believe in praying before planning and not planning before praying.

____You are valuable if you believe that the devil that hates you with a passion will soon respect your action.

____You are valuable if you are a person who believes that if you appreciate a person working with you or for you that person will increase in performance.

____ You are valuable if you know that wisdom that is not from above is dangerous.

_____You are valuable if you know how to give your employer or community what they cannot find elsewhere.

_____You are valuable if you know how to give your employee or group members what they cannot find elsewhere.

_____You are valuable if you learn that a wealth of experience awaits you, if you start at the bottom and grow to the top.

_____You are valuable if you believe that success without God is on the surface and distinctly superficial.

_____ You are valuable if you tell your problems only to the one who can do something about it.

_____You are valuable if you are a person that cares about fellow human beings.

_____You are valuable if you are proud of whom you selected as mentors. Reevaluate if you absolutely believe that your mentor is not valuable.

_____You are valuable if you are a person, manager, coach, and/or leader who knows how to effectively get all players in your group to play together for achieving one purpose which is winning.

____You are valuable if you know how to encourage others.

____Valuable people realize that their level of obedience determines their level of acquisition.

____You are valuable if you know that you do not always find what you are looking for the first time.

____You are valuable if know that the plan is meaningless until it is actually implemented.

____You are valuable if you know that what you say is as important as what you do.

____You are valuable if you do not let your inability overshadow your ability.

____You are valuable if you love your neighbor

____You are valuable if you give prayer to others.

____You are valuable if you know that the first to think of an idea may not be the first to reap the result of putting the idea to action.

____You are valuable if you know that mistakes are overly regrettable if nothing is learned from the mistake.

____ You are valuable if you know that tomorrow is another blessed day.

____You are valuable if you know that a real knockout occurs when you cannot get up again.

____You are valuable if you know that bad credit can change to good credit with time and discipline.

____You are valuable if you know that discouragement serves poverty of growth.

____You are valuable if you know that the first step to solving a problem is identifying the problem.

____You are valuable if you know that it is possible to get what you actually want through persistence.

____You are valuable if you realize that no question or idea is stupid.

____You are valuable if you do not depend on people to make you happy all the time.

____You are valuable if you know that the job you are doing right now is a higher level job for someone else.

____You are valuable if you believe that a good listener is always the preferred partner.

____You are valuable if you believe that a friend or relative when things are good should be a friend or relative when things are bad.

____Valuable people speak less when angry.

_____Valuable people write down their blessings.

_____Valuable people strive to improve on their character before improving on their reputation.

_____Valuable people do not take their problem from work to home.

_____Valuable people do not take their problem from home to work.

_____Valuable people believe that they are kings and queens for the things that they supply their group or family, and for the things they manage.

_____You are valuable if you believe that blessed are those who go out of their way to lessen others' burdens.

_____You are valuable if you believe that any level of education or job is better than none.

_____Valuable people are reliable people.

_____Valuable people do not let enviousness direct their actions.

_____Valuable people wear love as an emblem.

_____Valuable people realize that it is not always how fast the food is cooked but how well it is cooked.

____Valuable people know that the only way to become what you aspire is to start becoming.

____Valuable people know that you cannot plan and carry it out at the same time. Time for planning is definitely different from time for implementation.

____Valuable people know that people are drawn to ideologies that solve their problems.

____Valuable people spend more time on solutions than on problems.

____Valuable people channel their frustrations to positive actions.

____A valuable quote said, "But I know come tomorrow, with our plan directed by heaven, we'll praise; we'll laugh; and we'll sip on iced water."

____A valuable woman once said, "I may not be able to cook food like her, but I can at least boil water for her-I'll help with whatever my capacity allows."

____Valuable people do not ridicule those who cannot perform like them.

____Valuable people respect other cultures.

____In the abundance of word of God and words of inspiration the valuable increases in wisdom.

____Valuable people adjust their plan if there is a need to.

____Valuable people know that the degree of help and respect that they give to their parents and other leaders is the type that they will receive when their time comes.

____Valuable people prefer a straight dime, penny, or kobo any time, over a crooked dollar, pound, or naira. They prefer little through hard work than much through foul means.

____Valuable people prefer to be a small shot in friendly environment than being a big shot in unfriendly environment.

____Valuable people are proactive.

____Valuable people know that those businesses or ministries that are now 'mega' used to be 'mini'.

____Valuable people's importance is not based on what they accumulate but it is based on how many lives that they impact.

____Valuable people measure their status and class by their relationship with God.

____Valuable people do not downgrade any one in order to upgrade themselves.

_____A son that respects, prays, and communicates with his valuable father ends up being valuable.

_____A daughter that helps valuable mama in the kitchen all the time, ends up being a valuable cook, wife, and mama.

_____Valuable people believe that if you make God happy, He will make you happy.

_____A valuable verity goes, "Trust in the Lord with all thine heart; and lean not unto thine own understanding. In all thy ways acknowledge Him and He shall direct thy path." --Bible

_____The better you treat your constituents, employees, or family; the better you'll become.

_____ "A good head and a good heart are always a formidable combination." --Nelson Mandela

_____Valuable people will not betray you for money or position.

_____Valuable people believe that what goes into a child's head today helps to mold him or her for tomorrow.

_____Valuable people buy what they can afford and not what they cannot afford.

____Valuable people will never let the one percent insufficiency in their lives outshine the 99 percent sufficiency.

____The more you invest in education, the better you'll become.

____The way you solve other people's problems, the way you give to good causes, the way you support your group with time and money, and the way you help the less privileged are all your plan for meaningful success.

____The way you do the pluses and minuses to ensure that you spend less than you make is a plan to allow peace to reign in your house.

_____ "Let there be work, bread, water and salt for all."
--Nelson Mandela

Chapter 2

BECOMING A PEACE STRATEGIST

There are immeasurable gains that await peace makers and as such, you must continue to intensify your peace strategies. It means you will only succumb to the right solution and not yield to group A's solution unless group A is right. It is my personal observation that in group situations, it is almost impossible not to have what I call 'group A'. These are sometimes self-designated higher class of their total group that believes that it is either their way all the time or no way.

Group A can also emanate from people who love their group so much that they give their time, good sense of judgment, peacemaking knack, money, or other than the rest of the group. In a case like this, these individuals cannot help but to stand out among their group because they are valuable. It is not necessarily that they have ascribed status; rather, it is their flair and aptitude for doing things to help their group are factors that make them stand out in a good way.

My point is that not in all cases does group A believe that they are better in many ways than the rest of the group. You will find group A in communities, political circles, religious groups, work groups, professional organizations, and other settings. The negatively motivated group A   does not consult with the rest of the group when they make decisions yet they always expect 'group B' to join in bearing the burden and consequences of their decisions or actions. Almost in all cases, this group, by their action, usually ignites a fire of cold war that burns at the detriment of all in the total assemblage or in some cases at the expense of the masses that they represent.

To be effective against unconstructively inspired group A, it implies that you should not partake in meaningless wars and brouhahas for it deteriorates a true agenda and a sound vision. You must be peaceful, kind, and gentle with all in the group. You should be patient with your views and keep communicating until they start seeing certain things the way you see it. Be merciful when needed. Do not let anger control your actions all the time; be impartial to all in the group and others that your group influences or have authority over; always adjust if you believe that the way that you are going is wrong; and be firm on what you believe to be the right solution. You will still engage in meaningful debates and disagree when necessary for peace, which is essential for valuable endeavors is not actually the absence of disagreement.

Peacefulness is not actually being passive in what you have been called to do. Peace makers are hopeful and strong people. Peace makers understand that everybody in a group situation does not need to think alike. When all think alike, then no one is actually thinking or analyzing. Rather, peace is the presence of harmony, tranquility, and unity in meaningful endeavors. True peacemakers are never intimidated when it comes to doing right, for they realize that any plan strategized to slow them down usually translates to their goodness. They realize that any voice that unfairly rises against them shall be condemned spiritually; they also realize that no force can be against them in veracity, even when it appears so.

Harmony advocates are people with unlimited boundary for growth. Peace promoters choose this useful path because they realize that the principle of sowing and reaping stipulates that whatever you sow is what you reap. Consequently, if you sow seed of peace you will harvest products of peace.

Instead of carelessly becoming part of the fracas in your group with hope of getting compensated with title, money, promotion, or human coverage, try to position yourself as a harmony monger who only supports what is right before God and man. Harmony supporters find ways to bring concord and reconciliation among warring factions. They also forgive reasonably. When you swallow pride and forgive someone it makes you dignified and respectable .Moreover; it unclogs your line of prosperity.

It is obvious that in the process of trying to intensify your peace strategies, some people may call you undignified names but the truth of matter, is that you are the correctly aligned because you realize the ramifications of being a peacemaker; which include but are not limited to being called a prince or princess - the child of the greatest king. As a prince or princess in this highly dignified and special perspective, you should not settle for temporary peace measures like a cease fire.

Cease fire occurs when people put down guns and do not shoot for a while; when people working against you, give you momentary break; or when your enemies are asleep. Amazingly, genuine peace exists when wars are settled to the point that both parties become friends and unwilling to harm each other in any form. A cold war could be very dangerous to a society; that's the rationale for settling wars by addressing the issues that led to war. Also worthy of note is the fact that peace makers stay away from endeavors of revenge, viciousness, hate, and maliciousness.

It is also a business fact that investors and industrialists prefer to locate and invest in peaceful places. Similarly, successful people surround themselves with peaceful people. In actuality, true peace will not thrive in the absence of love; a good reason for us all to strengthen our love for each other.

Realize also that prosperous are those who love without demarcation, for such will brilliantly harvest from the flourishing gardens of diversity; and blessed also are those who have mastered their relationship with others different from them, for they shall see progress. Happy is that entity or board that loves not only their fraternity, sorority, tribal, religious, biological or other family, for they will see some harmony. Actually, what's needed is not partial harmony, but lasting peace which could only come from a "constant factor" and not "variable factors". This Constant Factor has, ad infinitum, given me peace in time of known and unknown wars. I call him 'merciful and holy' and my Bible calls Him Jesus, the Prince of Peace whose peace is continuous and incomparable to UNO's or other peace treaties. I share this information with my children and their friends, my church shares the same information in many ways, and I hope their schools will find ways to reinforce the teaching.

Chapter 3

TEACH MORE THAN ACADEMIC SUBJECTS

It is always encouraging and beneficial for any community when their leaders from diversified backgrounds come together meaningfully to discuss ways that the children of the community will benefit from their expertise that go beyond the academic subjects taught in the class room. For my own area it was obvious during the career planning program held at the Selma High School auditorium in August of 2013. I saw all types of community leaders who came with good intentions to be part of an honorable educational program. School officials were there, Chamber of Commerce was there, an economic development official was represented, the past mayor was there, the past chief of the fire department was there, city officials were there, federal and state house of representatives were there, my pastor and others pastors were there. Other offices and officials that I do not know had their representatives came; the main point here is that lots of community leaders who had the time, invitation, and other opportunities came. It is this type of cohesive village that undoubtedly raises a successful child.

When all these great leaders that a community has, come together for a good cause, they can offer their expertise or have their values or needs reflected in the school program. The verity is that parents play an extremely important role in conveying their values to their children through their personal teachings and those of the cultural and religious entities of their choice; still the public school and its support group are well situated to convey vital values, which include such important concepts, in our civil society, as fairness, responsibility, and respect for authority and other people.

Besides teaching the academic subjects that will enable people to thrive successfully in a society, students need to be taught about the bigger world around them. We as parents have this responsibility more than anybody else. Look, the world is massively getting diversified in terms of race, religion, ethnicity, and other ways people choose to affiliate themselves politically and religiously. Consequently, it is unlikely for people or the society as a whole to function normally without mutual respect for one another.

As a matter of certainty, schools then become places that proactively teach students about tolerating other cultures and consequently enjoying people who are different from them. There will never be anything wrong with students learning to love others different from them; that's God's way. My bible and mentors taught me that if a person has everything but lacks love and respect for others, that person is nothing.

As parents or mentors all over this world, there are lots of ways we can teach our students to love and respect others. My first choice is biblical teaching about love. Second, we have to teach our students or children to be good listeners. We teach them to pay attention to the good being said and not who is saying it or how it is being said. Third is teaching them about empathy. Empathy to me is a leadership trait that allows one to always, imaginatively, put himself in another person's shoes.

You can easily saturate your community with charismatic individuals by simply teaching your students, who are also your children, how to be kind, and how to make others feel respected and important. Charisma, as I proclaim in this book, is those good deeds or ways that make some people exceptionally attractive; people get drawn to them. I believe that much is invested when a child, in addition to academics, learns to be humble by not putting others down or taking credit for what God is doing, learns to respect others like them or not like them, learns to be empathetic, and learns how to outshine and outrival with an excellent spirit.

Chapter 4

CHARITY THAT BEGINS AT HOME IS A TREASURE

Excellent spirit entails strongly believing in something with positive influence so that all things will not distract you. It means not minding being ostracized or talked about when you are doing what's right. It means walking in love all the time. It means supporting what and where God gave you. Look, what is desired more than any thing is for people to do right by way of showing ourselves friendly to each other and desist, somehow, from activities that may hinder factual growth. When I write for the weekly column in our local newspaper or write for my books, I always find it pertinent to be practical with what I'm part of or what I know very well. Consequently, I will write a little bit about my community and its growth. I would love to see the motels, the restaurants, the grocery stores, the service stations, the barber shops, the dry cleaners, manufacturers, the mall, and etc. being impacted directly by our residents instead of helping our neighboring cities who have done the right things that breed growth. Do not get me wrong here, for there no wrong in sharing with neighboring communities, but any sharing that ignores home is questionable.

Productive people are those who hate not and fuss not about what they have not, but they love and are grateful for what they have and work hard to make it better or make the best out of it. Creative people endeavor to see hope not hopelessness, see good over evil; and they strongly believe that tomorrow is another blessed day, next week is another blessed week, next month is another blessed month, and next year is another blessed year.

It does not make sense to constantly reach out to support the outside when the inside is in dire need of what is being dished out to the outside. Charity begins at home; and it's true from all indications. I do not know how many mothers will reach out to breastfeed another hungry baby before breastfeeding her baby who cries for food. We cannot limit our seed or investment only to our backyard; still any financial status that is not felt in your abode or immediate community may be contentious. Do I believe that you should shop locally and sometimes shop outside? My answer is yes. Do I believe that you should support your family before supporting outside people? My answer is yes. Do I believe that you should pay a tithe and give offering to a home church before supporting another ministry? My answer is yes. Do I believe that we should support the stability of education in our area before helping other areas? Yes, I believe so.

Many times people do things to be recognized and commended publicly; at times people do extraordinary things by unnecessarily competing with others. Sometimes people take care of wants and overlook needs because they want to build up their reputation; the verity is that reputation, which is actually what people think about you, measures less in comparison to what God thinks about us or who we really are. Who we are is usually built based on personal choices that we make, values instilled by family and other influences like association, school, church, and et cetera.

In order to help build a well-thought-of character, a person's alliances or connections must not be a support group that tears down only. What people hear constantly about themselves affects them in a way. If you keep telling a child that he or she is obtuse or stupid, before long the child will start believing it. Conversely, if you keep telling a child that he or she is intelligent, before you know it that child starts thinking in that manner. We must not get tired in encouraging each other meaningfully instead of engaging in series of non-constructive criticisms. Constructive criticism is needed for shaping up; we cannot avoid that since humans are prone to making mistakes. Unwarranted discouragement and criticism actually deter people from bringing out their best. People become committed beyond expectation once they perceive a high level of appreciation for them. In every leadership position that we find ourselves, we must show examples that are worthy of emulation.

As a relative, neighbor, associate, church member, and a friend, I realize that we have to disagree at times, but when disagreement becomes the purpose for our meeting, our ultimate goal becomes colossally affected. Similarly, when politics, manipulations, and indecent maneuvering take center stage, the leaders ultimately become enemies to the people that they are assigned to help.

Some leaders or communities take appreciation and encouragement for all for granted and many times pay for it. It is overly beneficial to look beyond what makes people different if you want a cohesive and productive team. When all concerned realize that they are an essential part of the team, it leads to innovation, creativity, and the overall growth of the group or community. Pertinent, also, is the fact that encouragement reduces interpersonal conflicts as members feel less threatened. Consequently, productivity increases as less time and energy are spent on apologies and settling unnecessary disputes based on misunderstanding and misconception of each other.

I'm glad that my mentors and readers realize that a life of brouhaha achieves less in terms of improvement and overall growth but peace, love, and kindness make all things better. It bothers me sometimes when I'm told, "You have to understand that our community is so political." After all, there are lots of nice people in every community; I see lots of them in ours; and I see lots of hopeful people here too. Having abundance of anything is not enough; action is what produces results. Consequently, kindness, love, and hope must unite and strategize for a common goal so that true progress will emerge. True progress is usually possible when people realize who they are and what they want. Realistic personal assessment and evaluation gives room for realistic personal actions.

Chapter 5

DO A PERSONAL EVALUATION OF YOURSELF, FAMILY, AND ORGANIZATION

I believe that it is very dangerous to allow the enemy to grade you. If you don't ever grade or evaluate yourself and strategies, the enemy will mark you down by giving greater attention to your weaknesses and undermining your strength. Insecure people who have not learned how to hand their worries to God will always find ways to remind you of what you have not done or what they do better than you. Instead of instilling hope or offering help in their own way.

The preceding does not take away the importance of realistic and constructive evaluation which is meant to pinpoint areas that a person needs to work on for the family, community, employer, and other organizations for mutual benefit.

Significantly, a personal reason for the self-evaluation is to ascertain or pinpoint an area for my improvement-- whether we are talking about spiritual, administrative, personnel, instructional, sales, production, food, financial, publishing, and family matters. I know that it feels good to realize that, what you learned from your mistakes is helping you take care of business better in the present and in the future. Mistakes become disastrous if nothing is learned from it. I believe that we're learning from our mistakes.

One fact that I have realized and it is a concern to me is that some wise people keep their observation or evaluation to themselves simply because they do not have a designated title that defines them as leaders. But from my perspective, we are all leaders in away; you just have to develop your attributes. If you can initiate ideas, encourage or influence others to act or accomplish specific objectives, you are a leader. I do not think I have met any yet who cannot initiate an idea. Take time to read and study the four types of leaders that I have chosen for this piece. If one or more reminds you of who you are, then do your very best to keep practicing until you master your style. If you do not have the opportunity to practice it externally, start with your family and if it is done well, it will be noticeable and the external power or authority will reach out to you; sometimes you may not be able to know when or how they found out about your capability.

1. VISIONARY LEADERS - visionary leaders are great planners who have foresight, set attainable goals, and communicate shared vision. The most

important role for any entity is to establish a vision for the district, family, community and et cetera that reflects the consensus of the stakeholders. Vision is of immense importance to growth and prosperity. Without a vision, the bad can easily overthrow the good. Similarly, without a vision, the expenses can easily outweigh income. Without a vision, education may be displaced in the order of priority by a want. Furthermore, with a vision, wisdom, which starts with the fear of God, becomes essential. The book of Proverbs in the bible tells us that, "Where there is no vision the people perish."

2. MOTIVATIONAL LEADERS - are good listeners who talk and inspire others to action. If what the leaders are saying is meaningless to their team members, it is unlikely that the followers will act. In any setting, the vision and mission of the entity should be well conveyed to the stakeholders. As a school board member, we inspired almost the entire community to support the building of a new high school and it became a reality, and we will continue to utilize such skills in inspiring people to foster unity and respect, among each other, in our system.

3. ARCHETYPAL LEADER or LEADERSHIP BY EXAMPLE - demands that a leader approach a role from 'do as I do perspective'. Relative to

emulation, I love the fact that our board prays to Almighty God for direction before work sessions and meetings to emphasize the importance of God in all that we do. While praying is worthy of emulation, this piece does not encourage teachers or others to start their classes with praying. Remember what the book of Proverb says, "He that keepeth the law, happy is he." Success in leadership comes with patience. We know the law about praying in schools will be amended in the future, but until then you must utilize any opportunity, style, and venue to talk to God in school or at work. You do not have to pray out loud every time.

4. FACILITATORS/LEADERS WHO WALK IN LOVE - insure that everybody is heard and respected .The organization or group operates as a team. The group's goal is more important than people's differences. Be leaders who walk in love always. Value and respect what makes your team or family members different and consequently become a cohesive team. A cohesive team has greater chances of being successful and respected. We definitely want to be empathetic. Furthermore, realize that leaders who know what love is know how to conquer without unjustified wear and tear. Also admirable are leaders who do all in their best to ensure that

those coming behind will perform as good and better.

Chapter 6

CHOOSE MENTORS WISELY

My definitions of a good mentor are: First, that advisor who has attained a higher level of experience or knowledge in the career or interest that you are interested in. A person that you can genuinely look upon for advice and guidance. Second, a good mentor should be legitimately interested in your success. Third, an advisor who would not like to see you make the bad choices that he or she made. Fourth, stay away from advisors who achieves regardless of who gets hurt. Please, choose mentors that you don't mind attaining their type success but not less than they have achieved.

Watch and study your mentor to see what you'll learn. It is also pertinent to realize that your mentor is a human being who is susceptible to mistakes. As a result, you cannot let a mistake distract what you are learning. Evaluate not only your advisor's achievements but also under what circumstances he did or she achieve it. Time and technology changes affect almost all that we do these days. The most important is learning how your mentor relates to people and situations.

As a mentor, when things go wrong at times in my family I remind them that, we still have to remember that we are blessed and we must remain joyful. We must remain joyful, not because we fell or that because things went wrong but because we know that we will get up and keep growing.

Choose hopeful and optimistic mentors who believe in your ability to improve and succeed. Select mentors who believe that with God all things are possible. Do less with advisors who believe in stereotype in terms of achievement. By this, I mean people who are pessimistic and utterly negative. I am writing about people who believe that your height is a problem, your accent is a problem, your spirituality is the problem, your nationality is the issue, your color is a problem, your stature is a problem, your age is a problem, and your tolerance for other people and their culture is a problem. Regardless, I encourage you to keep searching until you find the right one. Do not settle for anybody that will guide you through the wrong path.

While performing a duty as a school board member, I was profoundly touched and flabbergasted when a concerned parent in our school system stated that her child needs a mentor because she had done all that she knows how in an effort to guide her child in the right direction. It was touching because it was too emotional for her, as her voice depicted accordingly. Personally, I believe she was thoughtful to have solicited the succor of a mentor because we all need guidance. In this case, the boy needs a man with experience and wisdom.

Sometimes it may be difficult for someone else to match children perfectly with mentors that they can physically be around with all the time. The values that a parent constantly tries to instill in a child will eventually make the child want to achieve the right way. A mentor is no more than a person looked up to for advice and direction. If a mentor is not within reach, there are satisfactory approaches that are readily available.

It may be wrong for a parent to constantly tell a child that he/she has to be like so and so. Some children will resist that because they prefer to be unique. Just tell the child that you have so much respect for a person for how he worked hard and sacrificed to achieve what this individual has achieved. Always include these two words, **sacrifice** and **hard work**. Most, if not all, emulate-able achievement are gained through hard work and sacrifice.

Remember, reiteration is for emphasis. If, for example, you continue to share with a child the characteristics that make Joseph, in the old testament of bible, one of the reputable individuals that lived on earth, before you know it, he will become the child's mentor. Joseph as a mentor will undoubtedly teach a mentee how to be focused when people that you trust disappoint you, will teach that it pays to forgive than to hold grudges, will teach that haters may be sent to help chart your destiny, will teach that you can achieve in your remote or present setting, and will teach that with God all things are possible. Above all, learning about Joseph will teach a child or anybody that it pays to have an excellent spirit.

Worthy of note, on the other hand, is the fact that Joseph achieved at a high level because he utilized the services of the greatest mentor who is omniscient, all-powerful, and ubiquitous.

During the interview process for a school Superintendent in 2008, I did the unusual but necessary when it was my time to speak. I emphatically told an interviewee that eventually got the job that the school system was looking for a superintendent who would look up to God, not politicians for direction, and act subsequently. I know I offended some people, but my assertion was from my heart; for I know then that the community was looking for a superintendent who would not affiliate with a political group. To me that translates to a person who puts his trust in God not man. More important is the fact that superintendents become mentors to lots of people as soon they are hired and as such you do not need just anybody in that position. You need someone who can absorb the heat, even, from some of his or her mentors; and seek direction from a God that knows it all.

Some mentors may intentionally criticize you in order to evaluate your heat absorption /response technique (HART) or get you to work harder, but take little or no advice from people ingrained in their parochial idiosyncrasies to the point that they always and intentionally demean you and, also, depict whatever makes you different from the next person as obstacle for success. Forget about what made you different from the next person and unite rigidly with hopeful people.

Chapter 7

WE HAVE TO UNITE

There are innumerable benefits that come from respecting and having confidence in what others specialize in. When you overlook people's differences and seek out their expertise, it assures productivity. From a business standpoint, it can increase your customer base. I know that people will support your venture if they realize that you advocate or stand for true unity and care less about their culture or looks.

Regardless of a person's credentials or good looks, your ability to excel as a local, state, national, or international leader is dependent upon your ability to work well with others, particularly those different from you. When you value other people's culture, or difference, the chances are great that you will gain their friendship, admiration, support and respect. The more united people are, the happier they become. People in the law enforcement, in the medical, in the government service, in teaching, and service industries should perform their duties so as to earn the respect of the public and the people that they serve. The issue of trust should be reciprocal particularly in the education arena.

As parents, it is imperative that we continue to have confidence in the teachers and administrators who take care of our children for that many hours a day while we are at work or at school. Moreover, it is absolutely necessary that teachers do not betray the huge trust delegated to them. A balance must be maintained and it demands the cooperation of both parties.

Furthermore, parents must continue to discourage animosity between our children and their valuable teachers, school administrators, Sunday school teachers, youth ministers, coaches, and pastors. When a child hates a teacher or other mentor, it affects his or her ability to learn effectively. Similarly, when a teacher hates a student it affects the learning capacity of that child. When a child brings a complaint home about a teacher, it is helpful to hear from the teacher too before concluding on what to do or not to do. More so, when you meet with the teacher, allow not your child to disrespect the teacher in your presence. Assure the teacher that your child has been taught not to disrespect the school and other respectable officials.

The caliber of training, assessment, and screening that teachers are supposed to undergo these days make it possible for a methodical School System to have a greater percentage of trustworthy teachers. Children are the dearest asset to a parent's heart and all concerned should treat them accordingly. For the teachers and mentors; anybody that is dutifully fulfilling his or her calling by helping to develop children deserves respect and should be accorded such. Regardless of how well packaged a school system or other sources of mentorship are, inappropriateness can still sift through. Any time that unsuitability or incongruity infiltrates a system the teachers and parents should team up and show their concern. It's our business to hamper any inappropriateness that is designed to interfere with the proper development of our children. There should be no biases in the way that parents perceive a teacher or in the way that a teacher treats a child. A principal said this emphatically to me, "In this school, I'm their mother and my two assistants are their fathers" I couldn't disagree with her based on my observation when myself and the President of the School Board did a tour of the school that she heads; because she knew the students very well. She knew the students that are doing well and the ones that need more attention in order to help them improve. Every student that we saw in the hallway she called by name and told us the student's standing. Not all parents know this aspect about the principal and other school officials; some just react negatively when their child is reprimanded without realizing that the reprimand is for the child's good.

When there are no uncertainties, reprimands do exactly what they are meant for; help the children. For example, as a parent, I have never encouraged lengthy suspensions or expulsions particularly, in the case where a child lives with   parents who go to work every day. My position is that you can end up doing the child more harm than good. In many cases, I believe that an alternative school should help the children and in some cases, reliable school officials should be allowed to discipline children in the school and discipline should be based on what a child did. Significantly, families should follow up from where the school stopped each day.

The fact that there are no perfect families should not negate the point that the most important values come from homes. With children, or even adults, mistakes are unavoidable and a teacher or a child should not be hated for reasonable disciplines; rather the behavior that got the child in trouble should be hated and attacked with all means necessary. When School officials and parents team up adequately, good citizens-well rounded people are produced. This can only be made possible by recognizing that children should also be taught more than just academic subjects.

Chapter 8

TEACH LOVE AS ACADEMIC SUBJECTS

It is interesting to note that more community leaders like the business leaders, civic groups, and clergy have elevated their interest in the growth of the community's children. More people should be encouraged to participate in the educational growth of their community. Every aspect of growth in the community is affected by the educational standards of a place.

Technological advancements and human improbable ambition are not at par with the greatest but affordable harmonizer known as Love; little wonder the world is in danger of all types of war, including nuclear. If I have the authority, I will mandate 'love' to be taught in schools. Love will be listed among some core disciplines like reading, writing, math, science, history and et cetera that make up the foundation of every child's education. What serves as a foundation to a person's education helps to mold such individual.

Nothing good comes easy; consequently, the possibility of love becoming part of the curriculum is dependent upon fervent prayers because some people may not be ready to abandon their pesky, antiquated aversion so that true love will reign.

People despise love when they are constantly partial in their dealings, when they are ingrained in enviousness, when they have no respect for some people, when they forgive not.

It is repugnant to heavenly and earthly justices when you think you are better and look down on others, when you hate people just like that, when you use your power to hurt the people that you have been assigned to help, and when you utterly abominate unity.

Regardless of how much a person knows, if you don't know love, you are still uninformed and ignorant to a humungous extent. Worthy of acknowledging, also, is the fact that education without love is a demarcation; dime with love is valuable than lots of funds with hate. A dime with hate is useless; a follower with love is treasured over a leader or follower with hate. A leader with love is better than a follower with hate. It is decorous to be a student/listener with love as well as a teacher/speaker with love.

 You can smartly master your relationship with others so that you work with them effectively .Conversely, love should not be affected by conditions and environment; it is a commandment that we must strictly adhere to. You may disagree with people that you love, but you should not plan evil against them.

Some leadership, bible knowledge, church, and human resources lessons have taught us valuables such as to be good listeners, to be empathetic; we also learned about role reversal, being open, and being an encourager. To be a good listener, you have to engage in communication. You cannot allow your perception about the speaker affect what you are hearing. You have to pay attention to what is said and not how it is said. Empathy allows you to imaginatively put yourself in another person's predicament. Similarly, role reversal allows you to be treated like you have been treating others. While these factors enhance relationship and could be partly love's ingredients, still it is not love if envy is tolerated, if vengeance dominates, if enmity and evil against another rule, if destruction is allowed over mercy, if people celebrate others' calamities, and if love is mimicked for temporary or manipulative purposes.

Besides teaching the academic subjects that will enable people to thrive successfully in a society, students need to be taught about the larger world around them. We as parents have this responsibility more than anybody else. Look, the world is very diverse in terms of race, religion, ethnicity and other ways people choose to affiliate themselves. Consequently, it is unlikely for people or the society as a whole to function normally without mutual respect for one another. The point has to be repeatedly emphasized because of its importance to the betterment of mankind and the entire world

As a matter of conviction, schools, churches, and homes then become places that teach students about tolerating other cultures and as a result enjoy people who are different from them. There will never be anything wrong with students learning to love others different from them; that's God's way. My bible and mentors taught me that if a person has everything but lacks love and respect for others, that person is nothing.

As a society, there are lots of ways we can teach our students to love and respect others. Again, my first option is biblical teaching about love. Second, we have to teach our students or children to be good listeners. We teach them to pay attention to the good being said and not who is saying it. Third is teaching them about the ability to understand and share feelings of another person. Empathy to me is a leadership trait that allows one to always, imaginatively, put himself in another person's shoes.

We can easily flood this world with individuals who are charming, fascinating, and strong in character by simply teaching our students, who are also our children or mentee, how to make others feel respected and important. Charming and valuable as I proclaim in this book are that good manners or ways that make some people remarkably attractive; people get drawn to them. I believe that much is invested when a child, in addition to academics, learns to be humble by not putting others down or taking credit for what God is doing; learns to respect others like them or not like them; learns to be empathetic; learns about the benefits of having an excellent spirit, and also the importance of good spiritual foundation .The significance of solid spiritual foundation can never be overemphasized. Bible knowledge actually enhances proper development and reduces crime.

Chapter 9

BIBLICAL KNOWLEDGE REDUCES CRIME

Many times I have wished that I have an individual power as a citizen, parents, or school board member to force a change in our system's curriculum but inopportunely it is not possible. The governance act (Act No. 2012-221) explains a Board of Education to mean "the legally constituted body that governs a local school, system promotes students learning and prepares students to be college and career ready." The act stipulates that the School Board and not individual members are delegated with governance responsibilities. If one board member has absolute authority, I would have made Bible Study very prominent, with minimal consultation, in our public schools.

I still reminisce my high school days when our Bible Knowledge (BK) teacher would structurally teach us bible as a subject. We did not pay much attention to him then which I regretted later in life. Although he taught the subject very well but more as a History or English Literature teacher than a pastor, Sunday school teacher, youth minister, evangelist, pope, and etc. would; still we learned true stories of how God deals with people; we heard and read about Jesus, Moses, Joseph, Abraham,

David, Daniel, Solomon, Esther, the virgin Mary, Elizabeth, Saul/Paul, Elijah, Goliath, Nebuchadnezzar, and more; we also heard about prayer and its effects. The teacher, for once, never told us to repent, forgive, and love others; but we heard stories and strategies that were superbly designed to impact a person for life, if attention is paid to the theme. For some of us that belonged to churches then, it helped more on Sundays when biblical teachings were reiterated with a spiritual anointing.

Bible knowledge has been and will continue to be utilized as a crime reduction Plan (CRP) during the Christmas season or other times that people perceive it as an obligation to give. Some of these seasons are special for us. They bring lots of blessings and joy; unfortunately statistics has it that crime of theft escalates during some of these seasons. Crime escalation likely comes from the fact that some people feel obligated to buy, expensive gifts that they cannot afford. Amazingly, there are many stories and teachings in the Bible that teach people to live a grateful life, be contented, and operate with the resources that are available to you. Check out this bible story; Peter and John went to pray in the temple and at the gate they saw a crippled man who begs for money. Peter said to the crippled, "silver and gold I do not have but what I have I give you, in the name of Jesus Christ, rise up and walk." He lifted the crippled and the man received strength and walked.

There are more stories in the Bible that exemplify the importance and the benefits of giving from your strength (what you have).A penny gift from a good source is better than a dollar from a bad source. Give your good gifts and don't worry about the next giver; after all, the best giver (God) is still incomparable and the greatest gift (Jesus) will never be matched.

I do not understand why people look down on Christmas cards or other cards but I know they are effective. If what is written on the card is not enough for you to depict how you feel, write more. You are giving when you love people indiscriminately, like Jesus, by going about doing good things and not hurting people. Shake hands, make people smile and laugh, and be selective in your hugging; for things are changing.

Let not human insatiable wants dictate the energy in what we give as we look forward to being a blessing to each other year round. I have come to the realization that one of the best gift that a parent can give a child or mentee is character education. Every activity may not require academics to properly function but every activity needs your character.

Chapter 10

CHARACTER EDUCATION IS IMPORTANT

We must teach our community's children that it is more beneficial to achieve at valuable costs than at any costs necessary. From my perspective, character education and math/reading are like two sides of a coin of which each side is needed in order to become valuable. We are strengthening the character of our community by ensuring that our students also learn about core values that are centered on empathy, hard work, caring relationships, respect for others, and meaningful acquisitions.

Do not get me wrong, reading and math are important to mankind in today's world but what is of extreme importance is the type of person doing that science, math, and reading those books. I know most people are doing their best relative to character education. This chapter is not about what is not being done, rather it is about what needs to be intensified and embraced by everybody.

Most school systems that are committed to character education endeavor to become the microcosm of a loving, civil, respectful, and peaceful community. They achieve this by developing meaningful and caring relationships among students and between school and families. It bothers me when parents perceive us (School Board) as antagonist when we should be partners. It also bothers me when parents' concerns are not properly addressed. We must be empathetic to each other's feelings, particularly relative to our student who is also a parent's child. For example, if we need nurses to help a sick student, we just need nurses to help a sick child and this should never result to fight between school and a parent because the sick child is the community's child. If a child needs special education services, the child needs it and with the school authority and parents being patient with each other, the child will get adequate services. When parents and school officials fight unnecessarily over a child, it sometimes put the child in difficult situation.

The truth is that caring relationships promote the desire to learn and the aspiration to be a good person. Similarly, when school and parents respect each other properly, this value is likely to be passed down to the student/child through the staff and the parents. Character building is ongoing and we are all affected. The more people improve in character the better their society becomes. A community that cares enjoys peace and love in their council meetings, in their school board meetings, classrooms, school corridors, churches, school bus, principal's office, parks, hospitals, and shopping centers.

Some behavioral scientists and some psychologists may disagree with me on this, but as a Christian, I stalwartly believe that there is no substitute to using God or our Lord Jesus Christ in building character. Fear and love of God instill empathy in people. The reason that people intentionally hurt others is the fact they care less about the offendee's feelings. But when you begin to internalize another's pain, you begin to desist from hurting them. One of the first thing a child or a person learns when you introduce God to them is creation in the book of Genesis. When you learn and believe in creation, the likelihood of respecting another human being, regardless of what makes you different becomes inevitable. When a child trusts in God, the child is likely to be focused and hopeful on God even when things do not go his or her way. No motivational speech is comparable to getting a child to accept Jesus and believe that greater is Lord that he/she has than any evil arrow thrown at him/her. A student that believes that God shall supply all needs will not do wrong when the supplied needs have not yet arrived. A God fearing student forgives others' trespasses as God forgives him/her too. A community like ours that is saturated with churches and temples must see the good that we are blessed with and consequently take advantage the good.

82

Chapter 11

SEE GOOD IN OTHERS & THINGS YOU'RE A PART OF

We have to see good in others and things we're part of. If what you are part of is 100% bad, no doubt, you are bad yourself. Some constantly insinuate abominable news about their employer, job, coworkers, school, associates, church, city, and even their own community.

Edification or constructive criticism is useful but habitual negativity is useless and perfectly tantamount with despondency. Being negative all the time positions a suggestion or argument as unpersuasive and renders, even, a meaningful observation as superficial and obiter dicta. We have to remain objective about people and places that God gave us so that more and better will follow accordingly. Just see good and bad will take care of itself.

Be careful with those who claim to care but relentlessly remind you of areas that they call your weaknesses. They come to you as faultless and better. These are downgrading forces that steal the joy needed for you to feel good about yourself and be grateful to God. These forces should not be taken for granted; still, they should not be overly recognized or overestimated because their strategy is inferior to our God's. The people that continuously point at others weaknesses or deficiencies are people who have not learned to properly deal with their insecurities by handing it over to God. They think that by putting you down, they have automatically upgraded themselves. This approach never works. What actually work are these teachings, "For the same measure that ye mete withal it shall be measured to you." and "let us not be weary in well doing, for in due season we shall reap, if we faint not." Friends and family, it's good to be good. We cannot be weary in supporting quality education and safety for all children, ensuring that the food on their table is also safe, and that they are taught that nobody, association, power, or board is greater than God.

Don't allow unworthy growth impeders to make you become too critical of yourself or what you are part of because it will negatively impinge on your life, and that's their purpose. Celebrate every blessing and victory regardless of how small and leave the rest to God. Celebrate others' success too because the way maker is still making a way; yours is coming at the right time. Say bye to unhealthy competition and doom forecasters and enjoy what you have and the more than enough that's imminent.

Relying on human being all the time to encourage you to keep moving on may be wrong. Insecurity, enviousness, and selfishness are capable of transforming people to degraders who usually react unconstructively to what God is doing around you. We are supposed to encourage each other but if they refuse to encourage you, keep encouraging them, others, and yourself and let the outcome be their problem. Encouraging others is the right thing to do and we must persist with it regardless of what we are going through. It is not a way of life that should fluctuate and as a result we are sticking to it.

Chapter 12

PERSISTING WITH THE RIGHT

I have met lot of good people in this world. I mean very kind and generous people; and you know some of these people without my endeavoring to list their names. These people, many times, make me thank God for putting them along my path of life and blessing me with them. Some bring out my smile whenever I see them, and some make me appreciate creation and the creatures. That's the power of love and all of us need to be engulfed by it for our continuous prosperity.

The verity is that how we treat people affects our plan regardless of how meticulous we are with our plan. We should be overwhelmed with trying to do well to others regardless of how bad they treat us. It is more beneficial to perceive wrong done to us as an experience than as a rationale to do evil or repay wrong. This chapter does not encourage those that initiate wrong doings; rather, it encourages the fact that stimulation of proper growth is possible through kindness, love, and forgiveness.

When you constantly react unconstructively to people who act differently toward you, you automatically give them control over your life. Amazingly, you can neutralize their evil ways through kindness. Moreover, when people behave differently, they most likely are going through hard times that may demand your attention, your help, and action. Instead of immersing yourself in revenge strategies, it may be best to see how you can make the person smile or laugh.

Mercy and forgiveness are powerful tools for getting over people's offenses against us. Trying to overcome evil with good is overly beneficial. Overcoming evil with good entails standing up for what is right all the time. For it is by doing so that you will be able to establish what is best for yourself and for the people you work for. Standing for what you believe is right may be uncomfortable at times but the truth is that if you continue to persevere, your situation will change for the best.

I write with the intention of helping to resolve world issues amicably so that lessons will be learned and wrong doings may be neutralized as much as possible. People should be able to separate some of my roles as a school board member or government official from other roles. When policy is made all we have to do is go along with it but still believe that the merciful should obtain mercy somehow. Regardless of how harsh a policy is, if you are a person that dishes out love and mercy, love and mercy will follow you regardless.

Occupying multiple positions with differing roles may
lead to a role conflict at times; but as far as I'm
concerned, there's no role conflict in well doing. A well-
intended person is a well-intended person, whether in a
board room, classroom, or off duty. Stand for right
everywhere, every time; think less about revenge, show
love and those people who has been cutting you short
will be amazed at your growth and possibly learn from a
simple but effective plan for a better life. Please be kind
and let's demolish those awkward boundaries that were
erected by cliques. Know ye also that your kindness may
be questionable if all that you do is select and help only
those in your clique. When you give only to those in
your group, you are only sowing a seed of division
which is likely to produce a harvest of division and
discord. Unfortunately, dissonance or unnecessary
conflicts are enemies of productive people.

Chapter 13

NOTHING MORE FRUITFUL THAN A PEACEFUL SEED

There is nothing more fruitful than a peaceful seed. Peaceful and productive results emanate from things done with purity of intention or with love for all in consideration. If a society invests wisely in education, the likelihood is very high that productive citizens will be produced. Productive translates to creative, industrious, prolific, and useful. When a group strategizes cohesively and purposefully, the outcome is usually remarkable, but group success can be negatively affected if members chase vain glory and provoke and envy others with disregard for the significance of unity.

Every decision making group should encourage input from all members and, then, analyze the advantages and disadvantages of every contribution before narrowing down on advantages that outweigh disadvantages. If you watch everyone in your group closely, you'll see that each is gifted but gifted differently. The leader who knows how to exploit the combined brilliance of the people in his or her group usually has a competitive edge over his or her rivals. Many times plans fail when a strategic plan is handled like a short term plan and vice versa, or when the cooperative brilliance of the group is not utilized.

While writing this chapter, I tried to conceal a chap stick on my desk in my palm by holding it tight with all five fingers and I was successful in protecting it; when I tried to hide it with only three fingers, half of the lip moisturizer was exposed. The lesson I learned from my demonstration was the verity that all five fingers, though dissimilar in appearance, are capable of achieving more if all team members work together for one goal.

Another good reason for respectfully getting all involved is that even if the outcome of a given project is unsatisfactory, everybody shares the blame; thereby, reducing fracas. Peace, which is essential for growth, gets adversely affected when disrespect takes center stage. Even a peace strategist gets offended if pushed too far, but still, your community needs more peacemakers.

Leadership positions come with power and power as far as I am concerned has to be managed, with the realization that power has to be shared. I believe that the true worth of power is measured by the overall purpose and effect of the power. If your power is fairness, respect, and love based, I bet you that productive power will follow you everywhere. Draw near to peace with your power, and peace will reciprocally draw near to you; don't undermine peace by seeing everything about the people or someone around you to be appalling or atrocious. Great strategists focus more on solutions than on weaknesses.

When you respect the people on your team and do not selfishly and unnecessarily rock the boat, your team members will respect you and make life easier for you. The team setting, as I write, includes your community or any group you are constantly part of. Mistakes can be a thing of past as we, all, position ourselves as peacemakers because of the earthly and heavenly benefits; peacemakers are high achievers who are called children of God.

Chapter 14

FORMING GOOD ASSOCIATION

I'm utterly encouraged that despite the current economic condition of this period, most productive people that I see or meet look like they belong to '*The Association of the Blessed and Highly Favored People*' or '*The Association of People Who Let God Fight Their Battles*'; or even '*The Association of Those That Fall and Get Back Up.*' I'm encouraged because these people that I'm talking about are not millionaires or financially richer than most in the community because I know what most do for a living, but they appear and show up like millionaires or people who have all problems solved. When you try to ask them how they are doing, you are bound to hear the answers like – "I'm blessed", "so far so good", "no need to complain", "my God shall supply my needs", "Tomorrow is even going to be better", "no weapon formed against me shall prosper", "favor is not fair", "God is good all time", "I'm better not bitter", and et cetera. If you have also known some of these people, don't get jealous at them; find out the force behind their ways and embrace the force.

Almost everybody is forming an association these days but that's not the rationale for my interest. Some associations get my attention based on their mission and vision. The majority of the associations that I'm writing about are not even registered. Regardless, be careful what you name your association, if you want it to be official, because it says a lot about the association. For some associations a name can, very well, serve as a mission and vision statement.

 Let's form, '*The Association of People Who Disagree but Hate Not.*' Some may think I'm trying to be funny, but this association will help to shed radiance to the fact that it is understandable and at times meaningful to disagree; still not hate. Disagreement becomes futile if nothing is learned from it. When we argue over an issue, it is pertinent that we not assume that our opponent is not capable of being right. When we are open when fighting for what we are certain to be right, it makes it possible for us to come up with a concrete solution. Many times have I amended or changed my position, despite stern disagreement, on issues in my businesses, in school board matters, in my job, church matters, in my family, and etc. just for the sake of openness to our overall mission and for the voice that matters most-God's voice. God is the only one whose yes today should be yes forever because He is omniscient-all knowing and ubiquitous.

Those who are familiar with my books or close to me know about my, *"Plan to unplan for effectiveness"* which stresses that it may be unwise to stick with a status quo or just the way things are even when they are no longer helpful. This approach is completely different from the ways of the so called, wishy washy people who constantly change position based on gains, environment, and fear of man, loss, & lack of God in the solution. Wishy washy people are unprincipled people who look up to man's favor instead of God's. In my opinion, they are more interested in how to get a position or office instead being interested in the true role of the office. When an issue or person's case come before us in our professional or nonprofessional capacity, it is easy for us to make conclusion based on what we already know. In the case of valuable people, they pray in addition to the ongoing prayer of God's people. While the prayer is going on, they endeavor to ascertain what God, the poor, and rich are saying. Moreover, they try to be empathetic by trying to put themselves in other person's shoes or imaginarily feel their pain." If the outcome of the internalization and waiting demands that they change their minds, they will change their minds. This does not mean that those in disagreement did not pray but it only assures the valuables of their roles in the situation in question.

When people disagree with you, particularly those not in your group, do not hate them and make decisions accordingly. Biased decisions can steal from any system and consequently deny them essential ingredients for proper growth. We must also not be jealous by any attention drawn by our colleagues or others but focus on our own strength for it is our own gift and uniqueness that will be instrumental to our consequential expansion. Everybody has a gift that can be developed for meaningful success but we must be grateful to God and be contented. If you are not satisfied, you may find it difficult to pay adequate attention to enhancing what you have.

Satisfaction comes from knowing yourself very well and being happy with who you are. It could be dangerous if do not love yourself. Do not always give others the opportunity to characterize you. Set your eyes on improvement and not on your past mistakes and what people think. See yourself as someone who is also equipped to excel in that particular endeavor that you're gifted on or passionate about.

Chapter 15

DEFINE YOUR OWN SELF

It is absolutely wrong to be comfortable with other
people's improper definition of you. It is utterly right for
you to define yourself and do so in a positive fashion.
Even places can define themselves and can only do so
through the citizens or occupants of those places. It is
divergent to the principles of growth and increase to see
yourself any less than God sees you. We, as God's
children, are part of this world and God never calls us
lower than or last on the list. Moreover I could not use
"bad" or "under" to categorize any school system or a
society   that has produced good high school students,
college students, good citizens, good parents, good
doctors, nurses, police officers, managers, firefighters,
lawyers, teachers, Superintendents, principals, engineers,
mayors, house of reps., chiefs, productive workers and
business people, good parents, good authors, great
artists, professionals, athletes, and etc.

But, we must realize that there's always room for
improvement, particularly, when outside observers or
experts see the need for improvement. You may not be
able to see it all, particularly, if you are not trained in
that specialty. A specialist may give his or her

evaluation's outcome a technical name or title that you officially accept but spiritually or personally reject so as not to start reasoning and thinking accordingly because as you think, so you are.

You do not have to accept what you are called in order to improve; just know that trimming, pruning, and pertinent adjustments are part of a growing process. Take reliable expert opinion but reject improper naming and hoodwinking from unreliable and so called expert opinion from a person or people who could also be bunch of bamboozlers.

When you are called underachiever or under developed and you accept such definitions, it makes it possible for you to compete in that manner. The more you hear it , the more you see yourself as not capable of producing things of value; or see yourself as a borrower or taker only instead of seeing yourself as a giver and achiever who is capable of maximizing the potential as the creator loaded.

For parents, it is gainful to define your child before somebody else unhelpfully does. Amazingly, there are outstanding people whom my family and I have personally gained from their decisions to always see good in us but constructively address our imperfections without bias. Good leaders and mentors have the tremendous ability to help bring the best and not the worst out of people. Even as of today, I know some people who still influence my direction by wisely reminding me that the future is brighter and that I can improve. None of us is perfect in every way and every day; so anyone that sees only the bad in you is a questionable influence for your life.

Other people's improper definition of you must be countered, and resisted positively without causing unnecessary brouhaha. In an effort to improve your life, some may call you 'greedy' 'insatiable' 'jack of all trades' 'acquisitive' avaricious'. You should call yourself 'ambitious' 'motivated' 'enterprising' 'God's servant'. The devil may call you a business with no hope of surviving this economy; call yourself a survivor, capable of surviving now and beyond and flourish like college football in the state of Alabama. Some people may call you 'unfit' for a position because of your difference; tell them that the Omniscient calls you a 'perfect fit' for the position.

Some may desire to put you down as somebody who does not speak much; tell them that productive people are usually identified by what they say and not how much they say or how they say it. Most valuable people that I have researched on prefer to be considered good listeners. Some may want to ridicule your small or big voice to the extent that they would not want you to be heard; let them know that such voice is special and only given to few extraordinary people by the Almighty. Some may call you 'weak' because of your effort to see people from different backgrounds work together, call yourself a child of God and a peace maker.

People may unjustifiably write you off because of your past mistakes; tell the so-called 'never failed' that you have learned so much from your mistakes that they constantly serve as a stepping stones. It was those mistakes that prepared you to become such an astute advisor, writer, and such a prudent a mentor. Remember, in many cases, you may not effectively teach what you lack experience in.

Teach others whatever good experience that you have in life and the things that you learned from bad experience; you will benefit from the principle of sowing and reaping which stipulates that what you sow is what you will reap. If you share what you know, others will share pertinent information to help you become better. For example, through my experiences and trainings in food safety, I have realized the importance of food safety and every September, which is the food safety education month, every summer when people cook outside a lot, every Thanksgiving and Christmas period when people cook a whole lot, I have utilized my column in our community's local newspaper to share about the importance of learning about food safety.

Chapter 16

FOOD SAFETY EDUCATION IS WORTHY

I'm soliciting the succor of all in the world in joining us in celebrating food safety awareness. As a Consumer Food Safety Protection Specialist, I know first-hand, the importance of food safety education and the perils of adulterated and contaminated foods. Food borne illness is a very serious public health risk and all of us are vulnerable. Reflect on the numbers: Each year, approximately 76 million cases of food-borne illness occur in the United States alone, according to the Centers for Disease Control and Prevention (CDC). Of those cases of food-borne illness, more than 325,000 people are hospitalized and about 5,000 people die – that is almost 13 people every day.

The truth is that children are among the groups that can easily be stricken by food borne illness. Typical symptoms of food poisoning, in the short term, include diarrhea, fever, abdominal cramps, vomiting; and long-term effects include kidney failure, chronic or reactive arthritis, brain and nerve damage and etc.

Some people are allergic to certain foods like soy, milk, fish, shellfish, tree nuts, wheat, eggs, etc. and I suggest they take precautionary measures and read labels because these 8 allergens are designated as "major food allergens" by the Food Allergen Labeling and Consumer Protection ACT (FALCPA) of 2004.

Pathogens like E.Coli O157:H7, Listeria Monocytogenes, Salmonella, Campylobacter, etc. are biological hazards of concern. Common pathogens may produce the toxin in food before it is eaten or produce the toxin in a person's intestine after it is eaten. Other examples of biological hazards include viruses which can be transferred easily in schools or at parties through people who are sick or food preparers who are sick. Parasites like Trichinella Spiralis and Trichinella Britovi can be transferred to human by eating undercooked pork or wild game infected with the parasite; which will consequently lead to a disease known as Trichinellosis or trichiniasis.

Chemical hazards include dishwashing detergents, pesticides or allergens that are used in food preparation. The physical hazards are physical objects like pins, piece of glass, etc. that can conceal themselves in food and consequently hurt a person. Keep the physical and chemical hazards away from food preparation areas.

Preventive measures include washing hands with soap after toilet use, after playing with your pet, after touching dirty objects or objects that a lot of people touch. Wash utensils and cutting boards before and after contact with raw meat, poultry, seafood, and eggs. Sneeze and cough not on food or people. If you're very sick, sneezes/coughs regularly, have open wound, shows evidence of communicable disease in transmissible stage, you need a clearance from your doctor or other specialists on when to prepare food.

Treat raw meat as a carrier of sickness causing organisms. Keep raw meat and poultry apart from foods that won't be cooked. Use different cutting boards for meat, poultry, seafood, and veggies. You can't tell it's done by how it looks! Use a food thermometer to be sure meat and poultry have reached a safe minimum internal temperature; 160 °F instant for beef, pork, veal, lamb; 165 °F instant for turkey, chicken, duck, goose. Chill leftovers and take out foods within 2 hours and keep the fridge at 40 °F or below to keep bacteria from growing. Chilling food properly is one of the most effective ways to reduce the risk of food-borne illness. A bacterium actually spreads fasted between 40 °F and 140 °F.

Friends and family, information is important and that's what education or training outfits are set up to do – share information. It is up to you to get it and increase in knowledge and power. Read newspapers and you'll amazed at how much you will increase in current affairs, politics, education, and religion. You cannot become permanently powerful or an authority in anything without knowledge. I have two degrees in Business

Administration and own two businesses and as a result, I share business knowledge and information at any opportunity that I have. It is my belief that every family should aspire to have business because there is a special confidence that come with knowing that a business is yours. You can utilize your business to showcase that talent or gift or leadership skill that your other job did not give you the opportunity to bring out. It may be a chance to give someone else a job; it may be an opportunity to pass down something tangible to the generation coming behind you; it may be an opportunity to become an integral part of your community because all the taxes you pay go a long way to support your city and county.

Chapter 17

TIPS ON EFFECTIVE BUSINESS START UP

Do   a good analysis of the business that you plan to go into. Try a business that you have some kind of background on or you are very passionate about. Do not go into business because someone else is doing well in it. Have a business plan stating how you will finance your business, your target customers, your location, and how you plan to manage your business.

The next step is choosing your business structure. You can choose Sole Proprietorship, Limited Liability Company, Cooperative, Corporation, Partnership, and S Corporation. Of the preceding, the easiest to form and the most basic of all is the Sole Proprietorship. Here, you are the only one that owns the business and you are accountable for the assets and liabilities.

It is important to understand the current, past, and may be future trends associated with the business that you are going into. It is important that you understand the factors affecting consumer behavior in the services or products that you supply. For instance, I know that sales go up in our fashion stores during graduation periods, during Easter period, and during Christmas periods. Knowledge of these trends helps us to be prepared with the necessary resources for these periods.

Once you have established your structure of business, register your business, obtain business licenses and permits, and try to know a little about the basics of business law and regulations affecting your business. Get the money for your business through grants, savings, and other. Borrow less when starting because of the unknown. Locate, hire employees if needed, and start.

Do your very best to be competitive and sell similar or more quality materials than your neighboring communities so that those that constantly spend their money outside will consider your business. I can assure you based on experience that there are a lot of people in your community who want you to succeed; who realize that your success is the community's success but there are few who will still allow the negative energy of enviousness steal from them.

Chapter 18

SUPPORT YOUR COMMUNITY

I believe that any person that works against his or her
community depicts a poverty of understanding. To love
your community and habitually shop outside your
community when such goods and services are in your
locality may be repugnant to the principle of normal
growth or even repulsive to the theory of plain
sanguinity and optimism.

It is improper to complain about the economic
deterioration of your community without doing anything
to help. God is pleased with helpers and not complainers.
One way of helping is by making a deliberate decision to
become an instrument of change for the good of your
area. Change as a matter of certainty is unlikely until the
wise of the community take up the challenges that they
face personally and confront such issues vehemently.

The truth of the matter is that when you shop in
your community, you boost the multiplier effect in such
community, for every dollar spent on goods, consulting,
and other services. Let's look at these results of spending
your dollar locally. First, you satisfied your reason for
such purchase. Second, you paid sales tax if applicable,
for helping your community. Third, the local business

that you supported paid taxes, rents, and licenses that help your people. Moreover, the business that you supported will be able to pay their employees and if the business keeps getting your support, it will increase pay for the employees, add more local employees, and even add benefits. Fourth, the employees will in turn support themselves and their families by buying food and other needs/wants locally, by paying house rents or house notes in the community, by supporting local churches and other local needs. Remember, the owners of the real estates and churches that these employees support are usually expected to prop up local agendas. The multiplier effects of your purchase and others may become overwhelming that your community booms and start attracting larger industries and other beneficial attentions. That's exactly the secrets behind the success of your neighboring towns.

Lack of information or knowledge can lead to the deterioration of a people. Do not allow lack of information to stop you from supporting local businesses, local churches, and local schools. Good industries attract workers in a place; and some of these workers come with school age children. One fact that you need to realize is that an increase in number for your local school's students translates to increase in fund-Money. When your units in public schools go up you get more financial support.

Again, complaining about what's wrong with your community is not the answer for growth. If you have the resources and connections to attract industries, attract industries. If you have the background or drive that can lead to a new business or businesses, open up a business, even at a diminutive level.

I do not know about you all but we have formulated a game plan to move our community forward and that's by paying less attention to evil forces and paying more attention to peace, love, and unity. We should not be afraid of doing well for we have God's power in us; we have God's love in us, and we have God's sound mind in us. The chains are utterly broken. The devil no longer holds our community hostage because we have, through peace & unity, withdrawn the name our community from the devil's register of deterioration, disintegration, and degeneration.

Chapter 19

YOUR COMMUNITY CAN BE GREAT

"Rome wasn't built in a day" is a popular saying that
substantiates the fact that planning and patience are
pertinent to lasting success. Instead of being immersed in
negativity, it is pertinent to pull from the positive that
your community is blessed with regardless of how
minute the resources seem. Most communities are going
global with what they can sell. The power to create
wealth has been given to us in the form of skills, gifts,
abilities, and other resources; and these have to be
properly managed before an individual or a community
can adequately benefit from it.

Every community must be encouraged to make excellent
use of their resources and thereby participate in the
international sharing. I know a community that has large
quantities of palm trees and is still poor when the world
utilizes products from palm tree to make wine, soap,
cream, lubricant, margarine, delicious palm oil, and
other foods.

It is either the verity that lack of knowledge or other
pertinent information denies the community their
growth; or the leaders and other community managers
lacks the know how to maximize the potential from their

resources; or the leaders pocket the gain in Swiss bank account where it does not benefit those that are blessed with the resources.

I have visited the modern day Rome, Italy twice and in trying to internalize and ask questions about the fact that thousands of people massively visit and bring money to the city from all over the world, I realized that the city that I currently live in has similar resources that could be maximized like Rome if politics gives way to prosperity. The similarities include, but not limited to, richness in history, richness in spirituality, richness in hospitality, and sumptuousness in fashion. These factors draw massive numbers of people, yearly, from May to August who go there to spend money as tourists. Accordingly, we shopped, visited restaurants, visited a fashion manufacturing industry, and visited historical sites. Remarkably, when my wife and I went to tour the prison where Apostle Peter and Paul were imprisoned, we were blessed to go in with a group, from Alabama, which we met at the entrance. Just meeting that group from the state we live in had me asking more questions.

I observed that when tourism is paid the deserved attention, it fetches large amount of money through goods and services associated with tourism. These services include transportation services, hospitality services, entertainment services, shopping, and etc. Sales tax climbs too.

What else could help the expansion of a place more than having a strong spiritual foundation? A church teaches responsibilities toward God, toward one another, toward authorities, and how to practically turn away from wicked ways. If these large numbers of churches in our communities keep teaching these effectively and the evidences continue to be obvious, there is no doubt to the fact that heaven will keep responding and our land will continue to expand accordingly.

Many people in my community are also gracious, particularly when politics takes back stage. I honestly do not believe that politics should affect God's commandment relative to love and how people treat one another. When love and friendliness are not in existence, peace diminishes. When peace shrinks, tourism and all that it draws becomes hugely affected.

Also evident is the fact that people in my community and surrounding areas are fashionable people. I see the interest and the looks of some people here and I'm sometimes flabbergasted that such looks are from small town people. The downtown stores, malls, and shopping centers are filled with fashion stores that people need to continue patronizing.

In view of all these, one can easily conclude that our community can be greater. Many times people see less fortune from what God blessed them with. I'm confident that mightier are what we have than some distractions that are repugnant to growth and stability; and I'm persuaded that God is capable of helping us in the right direction.

There is something special about an entity that knows about Fred Fiedler's contingency approach to management which stipulates that the efficient management of resources should be based on situation at hand and available resources; it should not be based on speculations, manipulations, assumptions, politics, and what everybody does. It is not about how much resources or talents; it is about the optimum utilization of available resources and profits. It is about catering for all in the community and not just a section. It is about realizing that power belongs to the people and not the politicians.

Chapter 20

EMULATE UDOKALAND

Land of Udoka is a lot of people's favorite place. This land is rich in culture, in religion, in love and in organizational structure. The people utilize praise and worship songs for cultural and religious festivities and for exercising / fitness; little wonder the land abound with good and fit looking human beings. For some reasons best known to them, they eat more fish than meat. When they eat meat they trim the fat off. They consume lots of vegetables and less of processed products. Their snacks are usually nuts and fruits.

Udoka is a democratic society in which party affiliation is not consolidated along tribal or racial lines. People belong to parties that cater to their needs. Votes are not divided between party lines. On the other hand, you do not have to vote with your party all the time, you just have to vote your conscience and your party will not ostracize or be offended by your action.

The citizens vote to elect leaders. They pray for leaders regularly and let God direct all works of the leaders. Under the Udoka constitution the leaders act as one and the individual Clan leader has no independent power. There is an unelected chief in the midst who ascends the throne without election but through customary essentials and God's approval. The Clan leaders also delegate all final endorsement to the chief of the Land. The Chief serves as the Clan Leader's adviser and interprets the needs of land to the leaders.

The growth and happiness of the residents of the land are the uttermost concern of this team. The team dwells less on weaknesses but focuses on strength; hate, power struggle and envy are forbidden. Love is so strong among this team that it became a model for the entire state. A land where nobody is encouraged to plan evil against other; a place where people will forgive your mistakes, particularly, if you deeply apologize and desist; a place where revenge has no chance; a place where love is taught as a subject in most of their schools; a place where peace makers are crowned regularly; a place where prayer and empathy are almost everybody's guidepost for decision making; and a place where people are judged by their actions and not assumptions. Udokas believe that power belongs to the people and not to the politicians. The politicians actually work for the People. It is correct to state that the Udokas love and respect democracy as Almighty directs.

Chapter 21

DEMOCRATIC LEADERSHIP STYLE

Democratic leadership style is the number one leadership style on my list of styles. I know that improvement and growth are inevitable once you allow democracy to reign supreme in leadership arrangements. Democratic leadership is for the people, by the people and of the people. I utterly distaste autocracy and oligarchy which are possible when one person or a small group or class governs and makes decisions to support their best interest and not what the masses want. It is very dangerous, particularly, if power and control are more important to the rulers than the betterment of their people. The essence of oligarchy is to amass wealth and form corrupt alliances. They do not believe that disagreement or not thinking alike is, sometimes, tolerable.

Most decision made at the top as a parent or other bodies that make decisions that affects children and students affect the children in one way or the other. For instance if the board does not collaborate effectively with the Superintendent and other stakeholders so that we can provide conducive learning and working environment, the students suffer. When programs, budget amendment, expense curtailment, school closures are done selfishly, the students suffer. These are applicable to every facet of leadership. Anytime the leaders are selfish driven, their people suffer.

Leaders represent their people and any resources for the land are supposed to be shared equitably. Leaders are not empowered to withhold good things from those that it is due when their efficacy is, also, measured by the degree of goodness, mercy, and vision that they do not interrupt.

Vision is setting a goal with the ability to foresee the good of the goal. The word vision comes from the Latin word *videre*, which is "to see." For instance, what do you see in fund increase for education in your society? Some may see unnecessary expenses; some may see students getting ahead in academics; some may see better jobs; some may see children who have quality education to be better generally in life; some see a city that's becoming attractive to industries because of increase in educated work force; some see students who are academically prepared to withstand the competition at four year college. A true leader cannot perceive investment in education as unnecessary expenses by looking for ways to diverge huge amount to disguised expenses that are setup to simply support the lavish habits that are evident in the lives of all corrupt officials. The leaders cannot continue to betray their responsibilities by amassing wealth and overlooking the poor people. Serious consequences await those that filch from the poor to support their pointless lifestyle.

Chapter 22

A COMMUNITY WITH EFFECTIVE LEADERS EXCELS

It is easy for leaders to get caught up with leadership theories learned in school and training that a person forgets the essentials of good leadership. An effective leader is simply a representative of the led. He or she works to satisfy the needs of his followers or team members. His people's peace, survival, and growth become his ultimate concern. Check this parable out: a certain couple went on a convention in another town, and left their 15 year old son in charge of his 3 sisters. This couple believed they left enough food to last their children until they are back. In addition, the father left money on his desk for use if need be. Above all, he wants to give approval via telephone before the money could be used.

Unexpectedly, the children ran out of bread, milk, meat, and juice. At midnight, the oldest son who could not stand the crying of his three sisters went to a nearby Wal-Mart and purchased the necessities. Due to circumstances, how late it was, and oversight, he forgot to ask for approval via phone because of the desperate situation in the house. Upon arrival home, the father realized that money was missing and questioned his son. The oldest son acknowledged using the money for needs while the parents were gone and went and presented a Walmart receipt for milk, bread, meat, and juice. To the amazement of all in the house, the father hugged his son and said, "Let's go to the back and play ball." While they were playing the father suddenly stopped, and in a stern voice reprimanded accordingly, "Next time, I don't want you to forget; find a way to tell me, but overall I'm proud of a son who took action when action has to be taken; at least we did not come home to starving and sick children." When the mother of the house heard what transpired in the back of the house, she was excited and went to the kitchen and prepared a steak dinner with ogbono soup; they prayed, ate, and went to bed peacefully and happily.

What I like about this story is the fact that both father and son exhibited the attributes of leaders who are motivated by love than by power, personal gain, & controlling spirit. Son left in Charge, did not utilize money to satisfy personal habit while his siblings were starving. He realized that a great leader takes care of his or people. That's exactly what true leadership is all about.

It would have been wrong for the father to ruthlessly punish a son who ran into a crisis and knew exactly what his priorities were. The father was a great leader too who knew how to budget money for the unexpected. Furthermore, he is the type of manager who takes the entire circumstances into account before making a decision or before unleashing an unwarranted reprimand.

Chapter 23

UTILIZING THE RIGHT WISDOM FOR EXCELLENCE

Even though today's world has some leaders that I respect and have learned from, still we need room for improvement because the potential for world leadership seems not to be maximized yet. If it is maximized we wouldn't have all these wars and economic crisis. Every society needs the right type of leaders to excel. History establishes that successful leaders know exactly how to balance the right wisdom with other acquired knowledge for successful management of their people or organization. While I was writing this piece, the US government was shut down because the Republicans and the Democrats were unable to agree on a spending plan for the fiscal year that started Tuesday October 1, 2003.

There is no doubt to me that US congress and the US President are top class leaders by the world's standards, but with this type of government shutdown that is likely to make more than 800,000 government workers to sit at home, makes me believe that there is room for improvement even at that level.

Economic expert like Brian Kessler estimates that a three to four week shutdown is likely to cost the economy $55 billion. Of concern also to me is the verity that the shutdown may not kill the Obamacare because the majority of the money for Obamacare comes from new taxes and fees and also from cost cuts to other programs like Medicare and other types of funding that is ongoing despite the government shut down.

There is not much that's worthy of emulation for me here since the congress will keep drawing their check; moreover, the president's salary of $400,000 will not be affected because it is considered a mandatory spending. I probably see it differently, but I have always thought that part of leadership is making sure that the people you lead have something and not positioning yourself to the point that the people you represent are denied while you have. These leaders, based on their background, know how to excel with the right wisdom and I'm surprised that they've allowed this issue to go so far.

One may be wondering what I mean by 'the right wisdom'. It is impossible for me to answer this without flaunting my religion, so bear with me. My Bible teaches me that there are types of wisdom. There is wisdom from Heaven and there is wisdom that is not from Heaven. The wisdom that is not from above is devilish, meaning that all of its approaches have the maneuvering, the scheming, and the deceitful mannerism of the devil.

This wisdom is also earthly and sensual; it is embedded with hatred, extreme enviousness; it is not peaceful; it is about worldly recognitions and acquisition; it's loaded with physical gratifications.

On the other hand, the wisdom from heaven is pure, peaceable, gentle, willing to yield, full of mercy and good fruits, without partiality, and without hypocrisy. To be peaceful, merciful, kind, respectful to others, able to yield when necessary, impartial, and firm on one's belief/position, is not weakness; it is wisdom from Above. I cannot see how and why this type of wisdom will fail any leader; It does not matter whether you are the President of a country or other entity, lawyer, judge, physician, director, coach, clergy, nurse, pharmacist, architect, computer specialist, a congressperson, parent, manager, school or education leader, federal government official, state official, county official, a city official, or any leader. The wisdom will ensure that you respect others working with you; this wisdom will ensure you become a good listener; this wisdom will ensure that you treat others the way you want to be treated; this wisdom will make you a helper instead of an oppressor; this wisdom make you empathetic; this wisdom will position you more as a giver than a taker; this wisdom will make you humble; this wisdom will persuade you to yield and reassess your style if your style is not fruitful. The ability to unplan when the original plan is no longer reasonable is a sound leadership peculiarity. There is no failing in this professional or leadership approach.

King Solomon of the bible, one of the greatest and richest leaders that ever existed believed that this leadership style would help him to improve even his Father's great Kingdom, so he went after this wisdom with all alacrity, and he got it. King Solomon was blessed by God and he excelled beyond expectations until arrogance, corruption, and disobedience set in and affected him adversely. If you are in a leadership position, just do what is right before God and man, and don't worry about the rest.

Advanced Policy & Decision Making theories or Six Sigma principles have their important roles in societies, but Jesus' leadership principles will not fail you because it is not a theory, hypothesis, or assumptions. Jesus is about facts and improvement. Jesus is solution oriented than problem oriented. When a problem arises, the focus is about solving and correcting than about blames. It is a leadership style that is meant to upgrade and not degrade. His style is designed to help the needy and give hope to people. A style that made Him accessible to the point that the poorest, the most humble, and children were drawn to Him. He always spoke in love and taught us the importance of being empathetic. His style will not condone bad, but will correct and forgive. Jesus participative leadership style is similar to the

Management by Objective (MBO) style, where
managers allow subordinates to be involved in decision
making that affects them. He always told His disciples
what to expect, how to react to situations, how and who
to pray to; and He encourages us to do what He did or
more. He prefers to lead as a friend or--what I also prefer
to call--team member. His style never thrives on
information breakdown. In summary, this style promotes
effective communication, trust, mercy, and cooperation
which are needed for any organization to function
superlatively.

Chapter 24

FOLLOW POLICY or MERCY

I respect effective judges because their jobs are not as easy as it seems particular, the spiritual or religious ones who harmonize between the law of the land and Jesus or God's principles. As a human being, it has not always been easy for me to find a balance between law/policy and mercy in terms of serving as a judge and jury in matters relative to school children and their future. When children who violate district's policies are brought before the School Board, it is not unusual to find yourself in an awkward position, particularly if you honestly see yourself representing God and mankind.

It is like most times that students who made mistake against our policy are brought before us, that I'm always taken   to the book of John chapter 8 of the bible where the Scribes and the Pharisees relied solely on the law while Jesus' approach, in the same case, taught us how to reprimand a person and still instill hope. According to the law, a lady who was caught in adultery was to be stoned .The law was extreme in the execution of judgment and flawed by objective because she could not have committed adultery by herself.

Similarly, when a child is found with a knife, razor, &
illegal drug, the child is suspended and brought before
the board for expulsion hearing while the drugs' source
or the child's bully remains unknown. Expulsion, even
as a Chief of Police consents, keeps sending the children
back to the street. Our policy calls for zero tolerance for
weapons and that's what a board member is meant to
vote on; but at times you are left to wonder why a child
would even come to school with a knife. No self-defense
excuse may justify bringing a gun to school. We want
students to report cases of bullying to their respective
teachers, counselors, assistant principals, and principals
instead of taking laws into their hand. I do not want a
student to be expelled and sent to street where he will
become worse in terms of learning how to become a
valuable citizen.

If the bullying appears not to stop, the parents should
follow protocols and keep appealing until it gets to the
superintendent's' desk.

No doubt that if an inexperienced child comes to school
with a weapon, it is likely that he or she will get caught.
Regardless of how the student pleads self-defense, the
student will be expelled. I hate to expel a student who
needs education but cannot effectively get it because an
experienced bully knows his or her game enough to
manipulate such sensitive situations.

I do not know exactly how the adulterous woman cried
to Jesus or what goes through the mind of children that
come before us, but the expressions on their faces,
always seem to sing the chorus of a song that pleads,
"I'm so sorry; Can you give me another chance; I'm so
sorry; Can you help shine my little light; help me help
me I want to stand."

We want these children to succeed regardless of
impediments; as we implement designs and policies that
are meant to help them defeat the obstacles on their path
to success. I applaud the Gang Resistance Education
Training Program (GREAT) and other proactive
programs. The school officials and resource officers who
follow school policy in doing their job are not the
enemy. Still, the sine qua non remains that we just need
to overlook politics and be sure that our plan is effective
because if children fail in getting education, we fail
collectively.

Leaders in all fields   made mistakes as children but wise
adults reprimanded them, stood up against the mistake
and helped them. Plan and policy reassessment is in no
way a weakness; it's a distinguished organizational
management strategy. I know a community that had a
very serious problem in terms of retaining their high
school and college graduates. When they reassessed their

plan and included few factors like working effectively with community's business leaders to ensure that they reach out more to local seniors as intern , the community began to blossom because most interns that did well with the firm are hired after internship and they spend most of their salary in the community.

Chapter 25

SIMPLE METHODS FOR RETAINING and ATTRACTING GRADUATES

May be your area needs more common sense plan for attracting and retaining graduates. When you constantly export college graduates to other communities, you categorically capitulate to the competition of human and intellectual capitals. Investing in education is equated to planting a seed for which a harvest is expected. During harvest, filtering or sifting becomes essential so that profitable and edible are kept as assets and return on investment. It is a blessing that the community that I live in have colleges like Concordia College, Selma University, Wallace Community College, and Judson College. I know your area is blessed also with good colleges but blessings become more evident when the best from these colleges are retained locally.

When trained and skilled workers are encouraged to stay in the community, they apply their skills and spend their money there. It is a germane common sense economics that has undoubtedly succored those who paid attention to it.

The recruitment of college graduates is becoming extremely competitive with the realization that the communities with lower than average educational attainment are being swallowed by communities with average and above educational attainment. It is a proven fact.

There are factors in a community that attract or make college students remain in the area that they graduated from. I know that quality of life is a factor. These young individuals are drawn to sound recreational activities like nice movie theaters, shopping centers, parks, restaurants, churches, and more. While these factors are important, the most important by far is job. Without dollar through the availability of job, college graduates or other assets are unlikely to stay or come to place.

Cost of living, is another factor that draws people. Peace, which we are all responsible for, and political stability are factors that can exert a pull on any person to a place. Established organizations in your area should be more open to internship for their graduates. It is a proven fact that more than 63 % of graduates who interned in a particular place decide to stay in the area.

Love and giving, boom and make a place alluring. My bible agrees and affirms in this manner, "Better is a dinner of herbs where love is, than a stalled ox and hatred therewith" If a place or person has most amenities but no love, still vital multiplying and proliferating factor is missing. Enviousness is an enemy to growth because it will deny you the benefits of prosperity which are based on giving, tithing, and supporting one another. Remember, money is not all that we should give. I do not know what I would have become or where I would have been if not for those pieces of advice given to me by my parents and some mentors. As a matter of fact, the advice is ongoing. Whatever positive mannerism that a person brings to his or her group is a gift. For instance, if you are a peacemaker, your peace making ability becomes a gift to your community or society.

Chapter 26

WHAT DO YOU BRING TO YOUR GROUP?

When I write or talk about giving, money readily comes to people's mind. Money, education and etc. are essential gifts but I'm writing about intangible gifts that are necessary for a better life, like words of encouragement and peaceful relationships.

I know this may sound strange to some people but when I went for an interview, before a City Council Officials, to become a Board of Education Member I did what was unusual. The interview went well, I thought, until one of the members asked me this question, "What would you bring to our school system?" I thought hard but the only answer that came to mind, which I gave, was the bible verse that I read in the bedroom before praying and going to the interview. I told her that I will bring fruit of the spirit which is love, joy, peace, longsuffering, kindness, goodness, faithfulness, gentleness, and self-control.

The committee members, I thought, looked at me strange, besides one lady who seemed not to have been bothered by my response. One member asked me about the information contained in the resume that I sent them and I said they are all my credentials .The same lady told me that the man sitting across is a preacher.

On my way home, I wondered if I blew an interview in that manner because Religion has its place and education has its place too. I should have known better, I kept telling myself. I was really hard on myself and somewhat felt that I did not prove anything. When I got home, I shared my experience with my wife and daughters who concurred by saying that if it was a mistake, it was certainly a good one. Amazingly, I had so much peace about the interview that I never talked about it. I was comfortable with any outcome; though not expecting much.

One morning, I went outside to pick up the newspaper and saw on the front page that I was appointed to the board. I rushed into the house singing, "When I think of His goodness and what He does for me, I can dance (7 times) all night!" My family wondered what was up, but I first told them to join the dance which they did, and eventually I shared the news. I was happy because I wanted to serve God and the community at that point as a School Board Member-- responsible for a forty-something million dollar annual budget, who are responsible for coming up with policies that ensure that children learn well in a good environment, and ensuring that the Superintendent, teachers and other staff do their best in a conducive environment. After much prayer, I felt that with a B.S. in Business Administration, Master's Degree in Educational Administration, Doctorate in Business Administration, plus fruits of the Spirit and God's support, I would be a good fit.

Do not be intimidated in giving what you have to your community or another even if it does not make sense to you or another because it may make sense to the Almighty; and if it makes sense to the Almighty, that means nothing can stop you.

Most times what you have may be exactly what is needed at that particular time. I know about a cripple who expected money from two men, but when the man gave what they have, the cripple moved from a crippled beggar to a man who walked around, praising God, & making his own money.

ABOUT THE AUTHOR

Dr. Udo F. Ufomadu is married to Rita Ufomadu. They have four children - Evelyn Ufomadu, Joy Ufomadu, Ezekiel Ufomadu, and Godson Ufomadu. He also has one grandson, Prince Ufomadu. Udo is a graduate of Troy State University, Alabama State University, and Madison University. He has been professionally trained at Texas A&M University and the University of Georgia. He is a Consumer Food Safety Protection Specialist with the Alabama Dept. of Agriculture/Industries. He is the author of seven books that are available at Amazon, eBay, Books-A-Million, Barnes and Noble, and etc. Udo is an award winning inspirational poet. He also writes inspirational songs. He is a member of Tabernacle of Praise Church in Selma, AL, and is a member of the Selma City Board of Education.

NOTES

www.an.eloueconomic.com

www.centerforpubliceducation.org

www.cnn.com

www.foodsafety.gov

New King James Version Bible

www.ingramcontent.com/pod-product-compliance
Lightning Source LLC
Chambersburg PA
CBHW021956090426
42811CB00001B/49